PRIVATE LESSONS

Stride HANON

By Peter Deneff

ISBN 0-634-09326-6

HAL•LEONARD®
CORPORATION

7777 W. BLUEMOUND RD. P.O. BOX 13819 MILWAUKEE, WI 53213

In Australia Contact:
Hal Leonard Australia Pty. Ltd.
4 Lentara Court
Cheltenham, Victoria, 3192 Australia
Email: ausadmin@halleonard.com

Visit Hal Leonard Online at
www.halleonard.com

for
George V. Deneff

About the author

Peter Deneff grew up in Long Beach, California listening to Greek and classical music and studying classical piano with Leaine Gibson. After starting his professional life playing in a Greek wedding band at age fifteen, he became obsessed with straight-ahead and Latin jazz. He began jazz studies with renowned pianist Mike Garson, where he crafted his art through studying some of the great jazz improvisers such as Charlie Parker, Bud Powell, and Chick Corea. During this time he also studied many ethnic styles that eventually led to the development of his classical and jazz compositional style as well as the formation of his Middle Eastern-Latin jazz group *Excursion (www.excursionjazz.com)*. He also pursued undergraduate and graduate studies in classical composition and film scoring at California State University Long Beach under the direction of Dr. Justus Matthews, Dr. Martin Herman and Perry Lamarca. Peter has written several best-selling books for Hal Leonard Corporation including *Jazz Hanon, Blues Hanon,* and *Salsa Hanon*. He has also composed and performed music for the Charles Sheen film, *Five Aces*. Deneff has performed at such varied venues as the Greek Theater, the Carpenter Performing Arts Center, the Playboy Jazz Festival, the Los Angeles Street Scene, the Orange County Street Fair, Universal Studios, the NAMM show, and the Baked Potato. His stylistic versatility has allowed him to play and/or sing with a diverse assortment of groups like Tierra, Ike Willis (singer with Frank Zappa), the Leslie Paula/Universal Studios Salsa Band, and Ebi, a notable Persian singer. Deneff also continues to play modern and folk Greek music for numerous events *(www.synthesimusic.com)* as well as an occasional Middle Eastern or jazz gig. Besides performing, Peter has also taught in many institutions such as Musician's Institute, Orange County High School of the Arts, and Cypress College, where he continues to teach classical and jazz piano. He spends most of his time in his studio producing projects for Yamaha Corporation *(Disklavier, Clavinova, Internet Direct Content)* and Hal Leonard Corporation *(PVG Play-Alongs, MI Press-Hanon Series)*.

Introduction

When one speaks of early jazz or American popular music, the subject of stride piano playing must invariably be mentioned. It is heard in its various incarnations in the ragtime music of Scott Joplin, the raucous stylings of Willie "The Lion" Smith, the bluesy and relaxed interpretations of Count Basie, the progressive and often dissonant sound of Thelonious Monk, as well as the syncopated and Latinized pyrotechnics of Michel Camilo. One can even watch an old Marx Brothers movie and find Chico Marx plunking away at a popular standard of his day, his left hand maintaining the steady stride rhythm while his right performs physical comedic feats. The ostinato two-beat feel of stride can also be found in the world of 19th and 20th century classical piano music. While perhaps it *"ain't got that swing,"* it certainly *does* mean a thing! In fact, while the rhythmic origins of swing music are undoubtedly rooted in Africa, the actual *bass-chord-bass-chord* technique of stride piano can be heard in the compositions of Romantic era pianists like Chopin and Liszt.

Perhaps the popularity of stride piano stems from the fact that the piano can provide a complete and self-contained accompaniment for itself or an ensemble. While jazz piano style is less bass-heavy and more reliant upon the bass player, the stride pianist often performs the function of the bass player as well as the accompanist and soloist. Because of the demanding nature of the left hand function in stride, there are significant physical challenges that must be overcome. This is where the exercises in this book offer their greatest value. These short studies were composed with the left hand in mind. When playing through them, the student will realize that this is a book that was primarily written to strengthen the left hand. This is not to say that the right hand will not be challenged by any means. On the contrary, the right hand parts are designed to create linear, contrapuntal, or syncopated melodic lines on top of the steadily chugging left hand.

As always, when practicing these exercises, there are a few pointers that should be kept in mind:

- Back should be straight with shoulders relaxed.
- Hands should be low profile with fingers curved.
- Always practice with a metronome.
- Tempo should be as fast as exercise can be performed accurately.
- Playing should be clean and even.
- Don't forget to breathe!

If one practices these studies with consistency, the physical demands of stride, ragtime, and even some classical repertoire will be more easily overcome. Of course, as in all disciplines, the student must enjoy the process as well as the results in order to be successful. So relax and enjoy practicing, learning, and attaining new levels of proficiency as you navigate through your lifelong journey of musical development.

Happy playing!
Peter Deneff

1

2

3

4

5

6

7

8

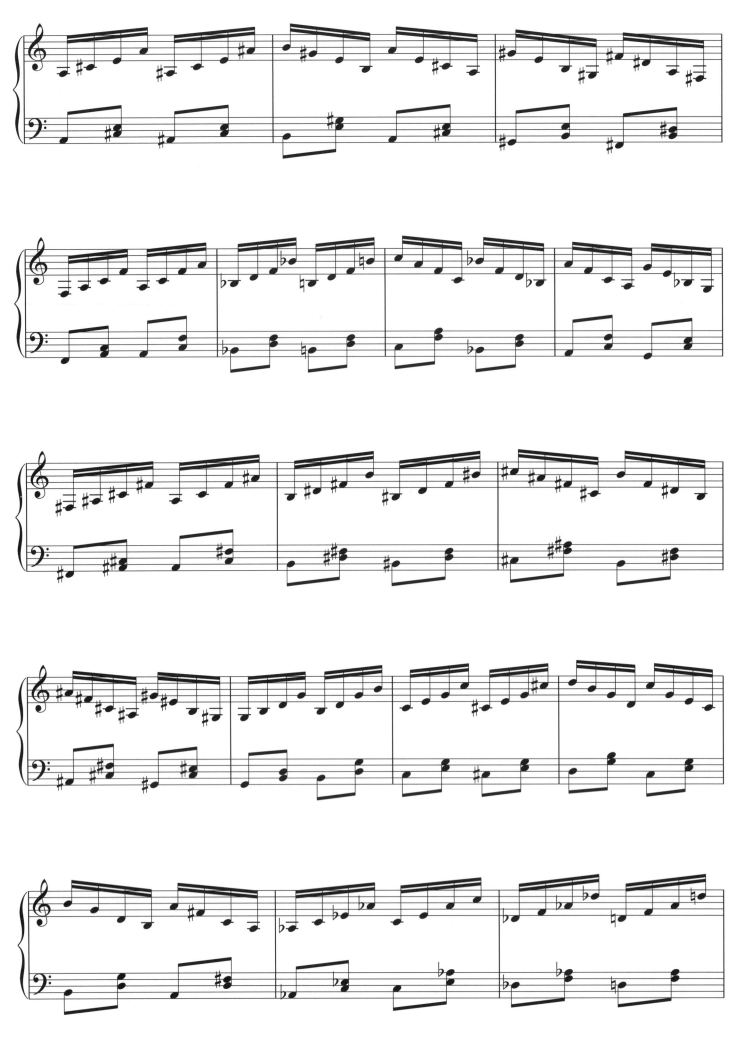

9

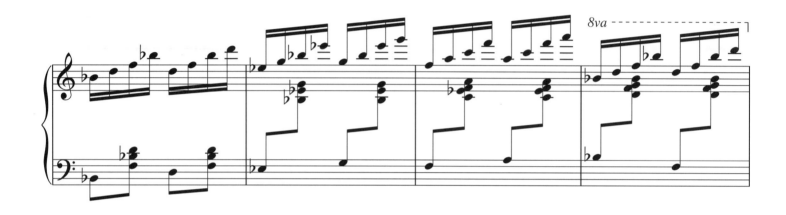

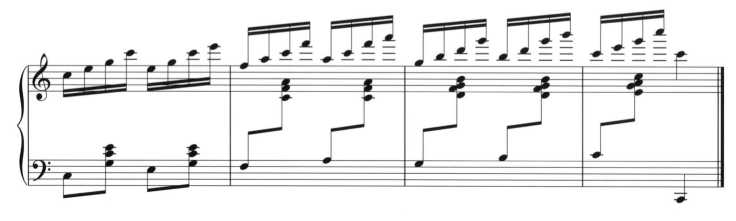

10

11

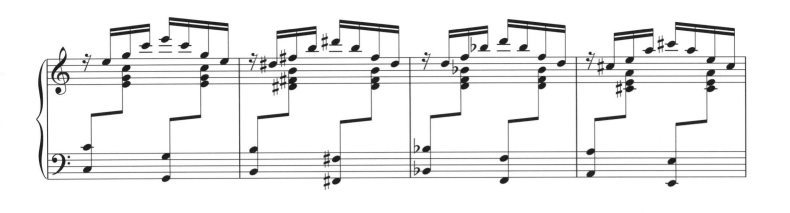

12

33

13

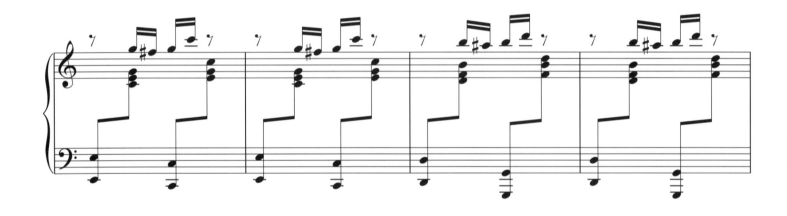

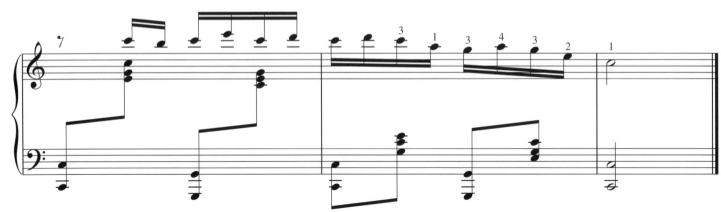

14

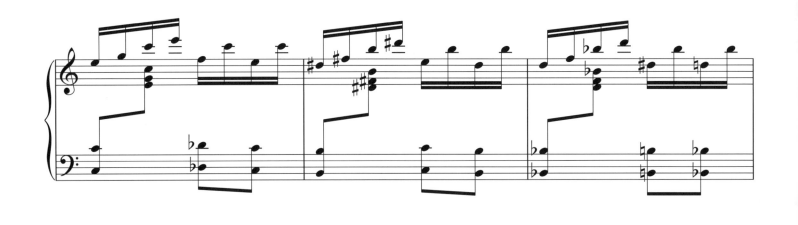

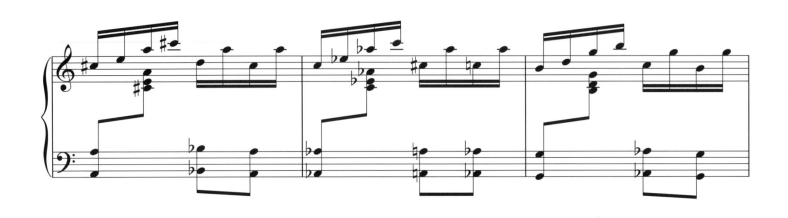

15

16

17

18

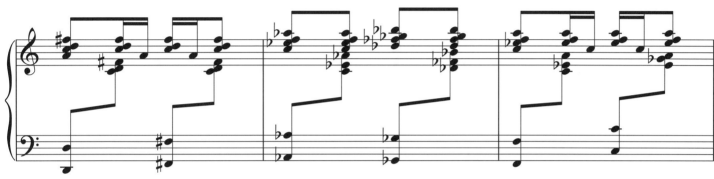

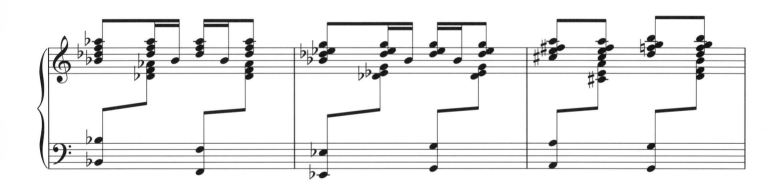

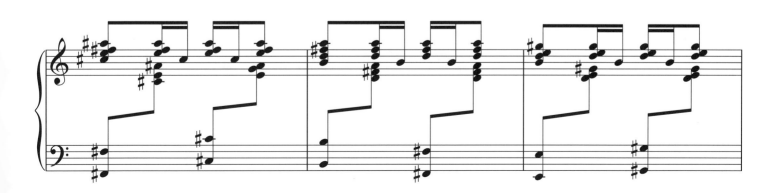

19

20

21

22

23

24

25

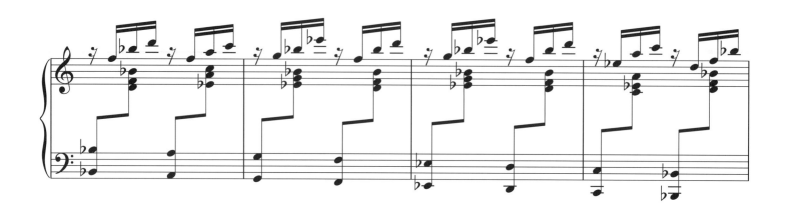

26

27

28

29

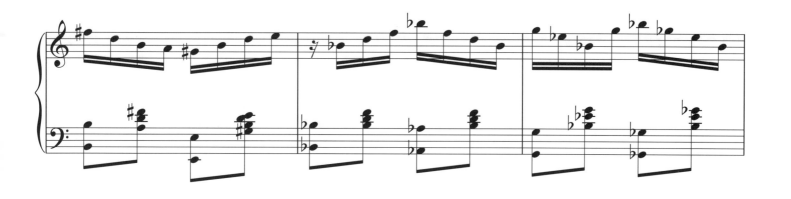

30

31

32

33

34

35

36

37

38

39

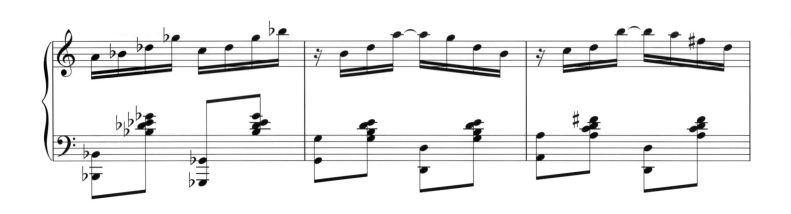

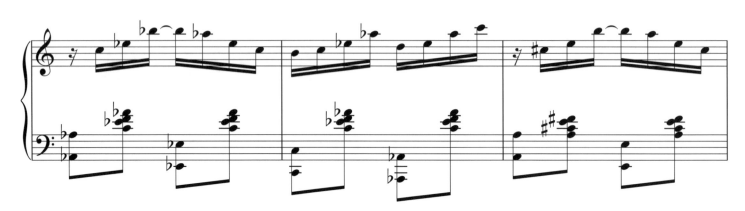

40

41

42

43

44

45

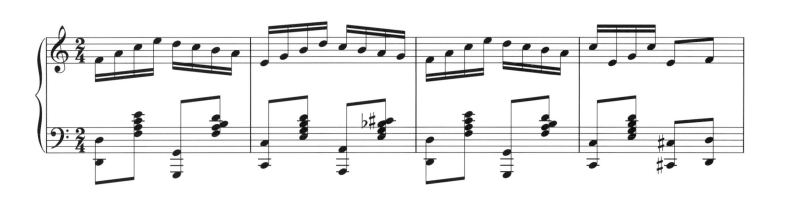

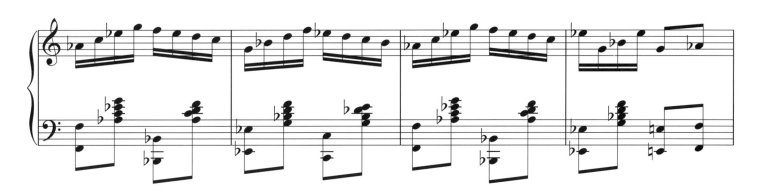

46

47

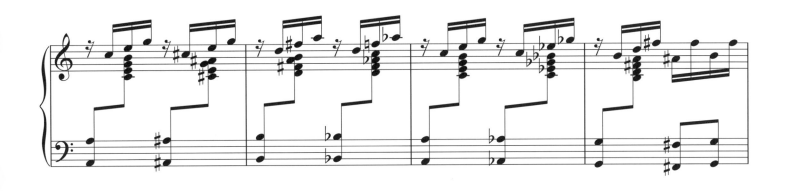

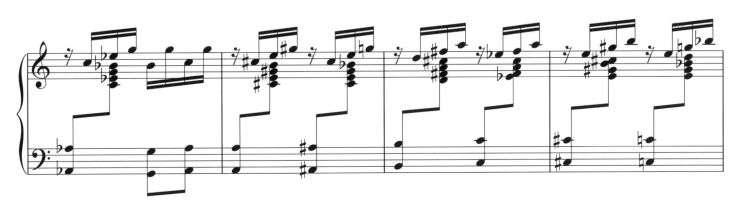

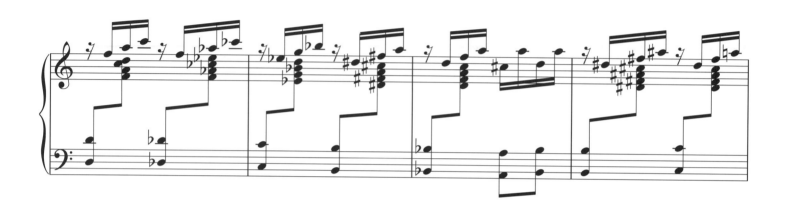

48

49

50

Musicians Institute Press

is the official series of Southern California's renowned music school, Musicians Institute. **MI** instructors, some of the finest musicians in the world, share their vast knowledge and experience with you – no matter what your current level. For guitar, bass, drums, vocals, and keyboards, **MI Press** offers the finest music curriculum for higher learning through a variety of series:

ESSENTIAL CONCEPTS
Designed from MI core curriculum programs.

MASTER CLASS
Designed from MI elective courses.

PRIVATE LESSONS
Tackle a variety of topics "one-on-one" with MI faculty instructors.

KEYBOARD

Blues Hanon
by Peter Deneff • Private Lessons
00695708 . . . . $14.95

Dictionary of Keyboard Grooves
by Gail Johnson • Private Lessons
00695556 Book/CD Pack $16.95

Funk Keyboards – The Complete Method
by Gail Johnson • Master Class
00695336 Book/CD Pack $14.95

Jazz Chord Hanon
by Peter Deneff • Private Lessons
00695791 . . . . $12.95

Jazz Hanon
by Peter Deneff • Private Lessons
00695554 . . . . $12.95

Jazz Piano
by Christian Klikovits • Essential Concepts
00695773 Book/CD Pack $17.95

Keyboard Technique
by Steve Weingard • Essential Concepts
00695365 . . . . $12.95

Keyboard Voicings
by Kevin King • Essential Concepts
00695209 . . . . $12.95

Music Reading for Keyboard
by Larry Steelman • Essential Concepts
00695205 . . . . $12.95

Pop Rock Keyboards
by Henry Sol-Eh Brewer & David Garfield • Private Lessons
00695509 Book/CD Pack $19.95

R&B Soul Keyboards
by Henry J. Brewer • Private Lessons
00695327 Book/CD Pack $16.95

Rock Hanon
by Peter Deneff • Private Lessons
00695784 . . . . $12.95

Salsa Hanon
by Peter Deneff • Private Lessons
00695226 . . . . $12.95

Stride Hanon
by Peter Deneff • Private Lessons
00695882 . . . . $12.95

DRUM

Afro-Cuban Coordination for Drumset
by Maria Martinez • Private Lessons
00695328 Book/CD Pack $14.95

Blues Drumming
by Ed Roscetti • Essential Concepts
00695623 Book/CD Pack $14.95

Brazilian Coordination for Drumset
by Maria Martinez • Master Class
00695284 Book/CD Pack $14.95

Chart Reading Workbook for Drummers
by Bobby Gabriele • Private Lessons
00695129 Book/CD Pack $14.95

Double Bass Drumming
by Jeff Bowders
00695723 Book/CD Pack $19.95

Drummer's Guide to Odd Meters
by Ed Roscetti • Essential Concepts
00695349 Book/CD Pack $14.95

Funk & Hip-Hop Grooves for Drums
by Ed Roscetti • Private Lessons
00695679 Book/CD Pack $14.95

Latin Soloing for Drumset
by Phil Maturano • Private Lessons
00695287 Book/CD Pack $14.95

Musician's Guide to Recording Drums
by Dallan Beck • Master Class
00695755 Book/CD Pack $19.95

Rock Drumming Workbook
by Ed Roscetti • Private Lessons
00695838 Book/CD Pack $19.95

Working the Inner Clock for Drumset
by Phil Maturano • Private Lessons
00695127 Book/CD Pack $16.95

FOR MORE INFORMATION, SEE YOUR LOCAL MUSIC DEALER,
OR WRITE TO:

HAL•LEONARD®
CORPORATION

7777 W. BLUEMOUND RD. P.O. BOX 13819 MILWAUKEE, WI 53213

Visit Hal Leonard Online at **www.halleonard.com**

VOICE

Harmony Vocals
by Mike Campbell & Tracee Lewis • Private Lessons
00695262 Book/CD Pack $17.95

Musician's Guide to Recording Vocals
by Dallan Beck • Private Lessons
00695626 Book/CD Pack $14.95

Sightsinging
by Mike Campbell • Essential Concepts
00695195 . . . . $17.95

Vocal Technique
by Dena Murray • Essential Concepts
00695427 Book/CD Pack $22.95

OTHER REFERENCE

Approach to Jazz Improvisation
by Dave Pozzi • Private Lessons
00695135 Book/CD Pack $17.95

Ear Training
by Keith Wyatt, Carl Schroeder & Joe Elliott •
Essential Concepts
00695198 Book/2-CD Pack $19.95

Encyclopedia of Reading Rhythms
by Gary Hess • Private Lessons
00695145 . . . . $19.95

Going Pro
by Kenny Kerner • Private Lessons
00695322 . . . . $17.95

Harmony & Theory
by Keith Wyatt & Carl Schroeder • Essential Concepts
00695161 . . . . $17.95

Home Recording Basics
featuring Dallan Beck
00695655 VHS Video $19.95

Lead Sheet Bible
by Robin Randall & Janice Peterson • Private Lessons
00695130 Book/CD Pack $19.95

Prices, contents, and availability subject to change without notice

0705

Jazz Instruction & Improvisation
Books for All Instruments from Hal Leonard

AN APPROACH TO JAZZ IMPROVISATION
by Dave Pozzi
Musicians Institute Press
Explore the styles of Charlie Parker, Sonny Rollins, Bud Powell and others with this comprehensive guide to jazz improvisation. Covers: scale choices • chord analysis • phrasing • melodies • harmonic progressions • more.
00695135 Book/CD Pack $17.95

BUILDING A JAZZ VOCABULARY
By Mike Steinel
A valuable resource for learning the basics of jazz from Mike Steinel of the University of North Texas. It covers: the basics of jazz • how to build effective solos • a comprehensive practice routine • and a jazz vocabulary of the masters.
00849911 ....$19.95

THE CYCLE OF FIFTHS
by Emile and Laura De Cosmo
This essential instruction book provides more than 450 exercises, including hundreds of melodic and rhythmic ideas. The book is designed to help improvisors master the cycle of fifths, one of the primary progressions in music. Guaranteed to refine technique, enhance improvisational fluency, and improve sight-reading!
00311114 ....$14.95

THE DIATONIC CYCLE
by Emile and Laura De Cosmo
Renowned jazz educators Emile and Laura De Cosmo provide more than 300 exercises to help improvisors tackle one of music's most common progressions: the diatonic cycle. This book is guaranteed to refine technique, enhance improvisational fluency, and improve sight-reading!
00311115 ....$16.95

EAR TRAINING
by Keith Wyatt, Carl Schroeder and Joe Elliott
Musicians Institute Press
Covers: basic pitch matching • singing major and minor scales • identifying intervals • transcribing melodies and rhythm • identifying chords and progressions • seventh chords and the blues • modal interchange, chromaticism, modulation • and more.
00695198 Book/2-CD Pack...................................$19.95

EXERCISES AND ETUDES FOR THE JAZZ INSTRUMENTALIST
by J.J. Johnson
Designed as study material and playable by any instrument, these pieces run the gamut of the jazz experience, featuring common and uncommon time signatures and keys, and styles from ballads to funk. They are progressively graded so that both beginners and professionals will be challenged by the demands of this wonderful music.
00842018 Bass Clef Edition...................................$16.95
00842042 Treble Clef Edition $16.95

JAZZOLOGY
THE ENCYCLOPEDIA OF JAZZ THEORY FOR ALL MUSICIANS
by Robert Rawlins and Nor Eddine Bahha
This comprehensive resource covers a variety of jazz topics, for beginners and pros of any instrument. The book serves as an encyclopedia for reference, a thorough methodology for the student, and a workbook for the classroom.
00311167 ....$17.95

JAZZ THEORY RESOURCES
by Bert Ligon
Houston Publishing, Inc.
This is a jazz theory text in two volumes. **Volume 1 includes:** review of basic theory • rhythm in jazz performance • triadic generalization • diatonic harmonic progressions and analysis • substitutions and turnarounds • and more. **Volume 2 includes:** modes and modal frameworks • quartal harmony • extended tertian structures and triadic superimposition • pentatonic applications • coloring "outside" the lines and beyond • and more.
00030458 Volume 1 ....$39.95
00030459 Volume 2 ....$29.95

JOY OF IMPROV
by Dave Frank and John Amaral
This book/CD course on improvisation for all instruments and all styles will help players develop monster musical skills! **Book One** imparts a solid basis in technique, rhythm, chord theory, ear training and improv concepts. **Book Two** explores more advanced chord voicings, chord arranging techniques and more challenging blues and melodic lines. The CD can be used as a listening and play-along tool.
00220005 Book 1 – Book/CD Pack $24.95
00220006 Book 2 – Book/CD Pack $24.95

THE PATH TO JAZZ IMPROVISATION
by Emile and Laura De Cosmo
This fascinating jazz instruction book offers an innovative, scholarly approach to the art of improvisation. It includes in-depth analysis and lessons about: cycle of fifths • diatonic cycle • overtone series • pentatonic scale • harmonic and melodic minor scale • polytonal order of keys • blues and bebop scales • modes • and more.
00310904 ....$14.95

THE SOURCE
THE DICTIONARY OF CONTEMPORARY AND TRADITIONAL SCALES
by Steve Barta
This book serves as an informative guide for people who are looking for good, solid information regarding scales, chords, and how they work together. It provides right and left hand fingerings for scales, chords, and complete inversions. Includes over 20 different scales, each written in all 12 keys.
00240885 ....$12.95

21 BEBOP EXERCISES
by Steve Rawlins
This book/CD pack is both a warm-up collection and a manual for bebop phrasing. Its tasty and sophisticated exercises will help you develop your proficiency with jazz interpretation. It concentrates on practice in all twelve keys – moving higher by half-step – to help develop dexterity and range. The companion CD includes all of the exercises in 12 keys.
00315341 Book/CD Pack $17.95

THE WOODSHEDDING SOURCE BOOK
by Emile De Cosmo
Rehearsing with this method daily will improve technique, reading ability, rhythmic and harmonic vocabulary, eye/finger coordination, endurance, range, theoretical knowledge, and listening skills – all of which lead to superior improvisational skills.
00842000 C Instruments $19.95

JAZZ PIANO

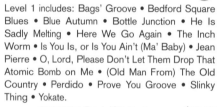

from A|B|R|S|M PUBLISHING

in Association with Hal Leonard Corporation.

> "What good is music if it ain't got that swing?"
>
> – Duke Ellington

The Associated Board responds with *Jazz Piano*, a comprehensive introduction to the world of jazz. A pioneering set of publications and optional assessment materials provide the building blocks you need to play jazz with imagination, understanding, and style, and to improvise effectively right from the start. Five levels of graded pieces contain a wide range of styles: funky jazz, up-tempo swing, calypso, Latin, jazz waltz, modal, bebop, Gospel, ragtime, free jazz, and more. There are classic tunes by Duke Ellington, Miles Davis, Bill Evans, and Thelonious Monk. Within each level there are 15 pieces, aural tests, quick studies, scales, arpeggios, and a CD with play-along tracks. The 15 pieces are presented in three categories: blues, standards, and contemporary jazz. Each piece provides a head/melody which contains all the characteristic voicings, phrasing, and rhythmic patterns needed for a stylish performance. An improvised section follows, where guideline pitches and left-hand voicings are given as a practical starting point for solos. Totally accessible and at the highest musical standards, these pieces provide the opportunity to play jazz confidently and creatively.

JAZZ PIANO – LEVEL 1

Level 1 includes: Bags' Groove • Bedford Square Blues • Blue Autumn • Bottle Junction • He Is Sadly Melting • Here We Go Again • The Inch Worm • Is You Is, or Is You Ain't (Ma' Baby) • Jean Pierre • O, Lord, Please Don't Let Them Drop That Atomic Bomb on Me • (Old Man From) The Old Country • Perdido • Prove You Groove • Slinky Thing • Yokate.

_____00290529 Book/CD Pack.............$12.95

JAZZ PIANO – LEVEL 2

Level 2 includes: Becky's Song • Big Noise from Winnetka • Blue Lullaby • C-Jam Blues • Contemplation • The Firefly • Good Time Blues • Hard Science • Moanin' • Now's the Time • On-Off Boogie • The Orchard • Softly as in a Morning Sunrise • St. Thomas • Swing It and C.

_____00290530 Book/CD Pack.............$12.95

JAZZ PIANO – LEVEL 3

Level 3 includes: Allfarthing Blues • Barrelhouse Blues • Birk's Works • Blues for Tom • Fly Me to the Moon (In Other Words) • I Wish I Knew How It Would Feel to Be Free • Neat Feet • The Peanut Vendor (El Manisero) • Sails • Saturday • A Smooth One • Sombrero Sam • Spanish Sketch • Swing Fun • Walking Blues.

_____00290531 Book/CD Pack...........$12.95

Prices, contents, and availability subject to change without notice.

FOR MORE INFORMATION, SEE YOUR LOCAL MUSIC DEALER, OR WRITE TO:

HAL•LEONARD® CORPORATION
7777 W. BLUEMOUND RD. P.O. BOX 13819 MILWAUKEE, WI 53213

Visit Hal Leonard Online at
www.halleonard.com

JAZZ PIANO – LEVEL 4

Level 4 includes: Blue Monk • Blues for Pete Johnson • Footprints • Freddie Freeloader • Heading Home • I'm Beginning to See the Light • Ikon (Memories of Ike) • In a Different Light • Lazy River • Nobody Knows the Trouble I've Seen • Original Rags • Oscar's Boogaloo • Shh! • Three-Four Blues • Undecided.

_____00290532 Book/CD Pack...........$12.95

JAZZ PIANO – LEVEL 5

Level 5 includes: All Blues • Blue Bossa • Chops • Christopher Columbus • Crossover Blues • Jamming with Jools • Lemon Cornette • Mambo Country • Oleo • An Oscar for Oscar • So Long • Take the "A" Train • That Monday Morning Feeling • Waltz for Autumn • 34 Skidoo.

_____00290533 Book/CD Pack...........$12.95

JAZZ PIANO FROM SCRATCH

Jazz Piano from Scratch is a complete step-by-step guide to playing jazz with confidence and style. Designed for the absolute beginner, it breaks down the process into simple yet fun activities, with many musical examples to illustrate the points made. The accompanying CD provides examples, activities, and some great trio playing to use as a backdrop to the student's own work. Together with a range of other supporting materials – pieces, scales, quick studies, aural tests and CDs – this book provides a comprehensive introduction to the world of jazz.

_____00290534 Book/CD Pack $24.95

1102